THE DAY MERCY WENT TO CHURCH

CAROLYN C. JOYCE

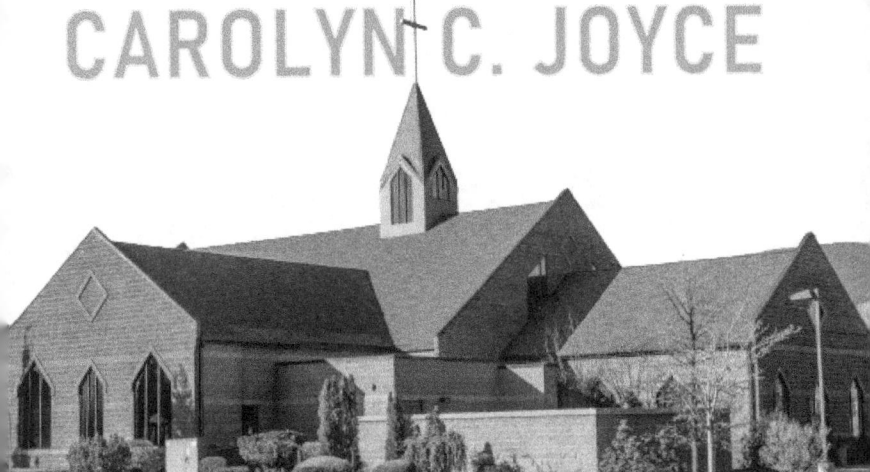

The Day Mercy Went To Church

Written by
Carolyn C. Joyce

The Glory Cloud publications

Sicklerville NJ

CAROLYN C. JOYCE

The Glory Cloud publications
PO Box 193
Sicklerville, NJ / 08081
www.theglorycloudpublications.com

Publisher's Note: This is a work of fiction. Names, characters,
places, and incidents are a product of the author's imagination.
Locales and public names are sometimes used for atmospheric
purposes. Although the main characters are based on real people,
the events they encounter may be exaggerated or fictitious. Any
other resemblance to actual people, living or dead, or to
businesses, companies, events, institutions, or locales is
completely coinci-dental.

Book Layout © 2017 BookDesignTemplates.com

The Day Mercy Went to Church / Carolyn C. Joyce. -- 1st ed.
paperback
ISBN 979-8-9859199-1-2

Contents

Dedication v

In Memory Of ix

Acknowledgements xi

Forward xvii

Prelude 1

Good Morning Abba Father! 3

Kiss On the Cheek 7

Pulling Up to the Church 13

Follow You All 17

Authority to Use My Power 21

The Day Mercy Went to Church (Poem) 25

About the Author 33

Dedication

I dedicate this book to:
My loving husband, Joseph Sr. (Joey)
My son, Joseph Jr. (Joe Joe)
My oldest grandson, Thamon
(Thame, Tha Tha)
My oldest granddaughter, Phaedra
My youngest grandchildren:
Gina, Legacy, and Joseph III (JW)

My siblings and siblings-in-love:
Pastor Lawrence (Larry) and Yvonne
Elder Terrence (Terry) and Dineall (Linda)
Kevin, Candace (Candy)
Heather, Wendall, Karen
Cherry, Michelle

My church family:
A Body of Caring People
Family Christian Fellowship

O give thanks unto the Lord; for he is good:
because his mercy endureth for ever.

PSALMS 118:1
THE HOLY BIBLE
(KJV)

In Memory Of

Our pritzy, tiny, 4-paw canine girly "Mitsey"

My caring, faithful, loving parents,
Reverend Eddie and Phyllis (Loretta) Clark

My beautiful, loving Auntie Inez

My amazing, merciful, tenderhearted 4-paw
feline son, Mercy
April 15, 2002 — November 27, 2020

My beautiful darling, precious daughter,
Tamika (Tammy)
July 06, 1974 — January 09, 2021

Acknowledgements

I have to start by thanking Abba Father, God, for it was He who caused His ability to become a possibility, where my flesh was saying impossible. And, Abba Father would say to me: "WITH ME, ALL THINGS ARE POSSIBLE." Thank you so much, Abba Father, for your Grace and Mercy that endures forever.

I'm shouting out this special thanks to you, my biological brother, prophet, writer, author, publisher: Terrence G. Clark, aka Elder Terry. As I was conversing with him one day about my well-known, talented feline son—Mercy—and how I would like to take Mercy to church. Terrence, you said: "That's a title for your book...do it."

Thank you so much, my beloved brother, for all the encouragement you have given me throughout the years. Thank you now for how you have made this opportunity for me to be published and released.

Brother—your books, magazines, articles, stories, and dramas have always kept me wondering if I could do what you do. I have a lot more to learn. Please know that you are one of my favorite authors, writers, etc. I love you, brother.

Thanks to my loving hubby, Joseph Sr., for not interrupting me (lol) and realizing that this book would be a blessing. Thank you, Joey, for all the things you do for me and most of all: loving me. I love you so much, Joey!

Thanks to my son, Joseph Jr. Joe Joe, your humbleness, your big heart of love that you always express to me; those anointed hugs you give; they cause the windows of Heaven to pour out a marvelous blessing. Son, you are so loved by your Momma. I love you very much, Joe Joe.

Thanks to my oldest grandchildren, Thamon and Phaedra. When I told them what

Uncle Terry had said, they responded immediately. "Momjae, nice...You can do it...do it!" Thanks for the encouragement and always showing how much you love me. You're my Kiddos, Thame and Phaedra. I love you so much!

Thanks to my younger grandchildren: Giana, Legacy, and Joseph III, aka J.W, for being special to me. The thoughts of our times together and the love I have for y'all helped me to do it. My little kiddos, I love you so much!

Thanks to my youngest brother, Kevin. Kevin, my 4-paw feline Mercy was from your 4-paw litter that mommy picked for me. Brother, you have encouraged me to walk in God's merciful Light Of Life.

Thanks to my sweet, sweet sister Candy. You have always been my baby girl and beautiful sister. Sis, even though you're fourteen years younger than me, you have been one of my great inspirators and a helpful encourager. You've grown to be a strong woman. Always remember, when God's Mercy speaks, it's a PAW TO THE FACE; a powerful anointed way to exceed in life, forever.

Candy, do you remember the night Mercy spoke to you? Pow with his paw! But, God gently said, Receive My Mercy—RMM. Stay focused, sister. God has so many blessings for you.

Thanks to my sisters and brothers that were given to me in a unique and special way. You all are special to me. There's no in-law, but there's In-Love. Do know that I Love You and will always love you. Pastor Yvonne, Sister Dineall (aka Linda), Karen, Cherry, Michelle, Heather, and Wendell.

Thanks to all my nieces and nephews who I love so much. You all make me feel so special. Mercy knew each one of you by name.

Also, thanks to my special moms—Mother Mary Fisher and Mrs. Gloria Smith. The love you give to your children and grandchildren encouraged me.

Thanks to my special aunt and uncle—Juanita Williams and Charles Bogan. God knew how to join Uncle Eddie to you, Aunt Juanita; and Aunt Darlene to you, Uncle Charles, and fit you into our family. Thank you for keeping their love alive.

Thanks to all my cousins and friends. Oh, how God has blessed us. We can go to one another and encourage each other in that time of need. And what you didn't know is: my time of need has encouraged me to stay focused.

And special thanks to Pastor Larry, Pastor Yvonne, all my FLCF family, and Sister Mary Waters. You all have helped me to make this book possible and may not have realized it. Its your concerns, your prayers, and your ministry of love that keeps me faithful to hear God's Word.

Be blessed and continue to be a blessing. Always be reminded that the Lord is good; His mercy is everlasting, and His truth endureth to all generations. (Psalm 100:5) I Love You!

Many thanks to the willing and talented Illustrator, James (Sonny) Pollard, who connected near the end of process, with The Glory Cloud publications, to help make this book a glorious, ecstatic read.

Also, thanks to my special granddaughter, Maritzabel. You always expect the best of me. I Love you.

In conclusion, an extra shout-out to my aforementioned "Pastor Larry" (my oldest brother). I could not begin my short story if I didn't give "special, special thanks" for all the years of blessings you brought to my life.

Pastor I'm so blessed by your gift of humility expressed in your message of love and hope for families all around the world.

Mercy would always sense the anointing upon your life. Did you know that whenever he heard your voice, he would immediately respond with a tender purr? I believe that merciful purr will continue to follow you anew every morning (lol). Please know that your phenomenal lifestyle has been a lesson for me. I love you, Big Bro!

Forward

It's somewhat of an allegory. In this short, lively tale, my sister Carolyn Joyce, "Lynny," her nickname, brings together the essence of a family, a church, and a furry friend.

The relationships families have with their pets vary in intimacy. Often, a horse, dog, a cat, a bird, a fish, a gerbil, etc., go far beyond just being playmates or wistful companionship but are found grafted into the family tree.

Some human and pet relationships flow so deep that the question arises: When the pet departs to the other side, will they be awaiting us, their human masters, in heaven?

Conceivably, pets are more than social investments. They become an expression of a family's nature. Perhaps not on a celestial level, but in many ways cherubic, pets are sent by God for those certain life encounters sometimes to absorb loneliness, and despair and to release, laughter, and joy.

What about a tabby named Mercy who had a destiny appointment to keep? And, despite the challenges of 2020, he would arrive either in the body or in spirit.

When my sister's little, grey-striped friend went home, I was asked the above question. My answer was yes. Without establishing a doctrine, I believe pets also become the embodiment of precious moments shared in a family. When they pass, they are there in Glory awaiting along with the one who gives life and is eternal.

Mercy's little voice translated from purrs and trills to the voice of God with a prolific word for not only my sister but to all to hear.

—Terrence G. Clark
Founder of VoiceCNC.com

Prelude

Oh, Mercy, Mercy, Mercy! You're always following me. You help me through my days with great love; the amazing things you do for me. I'll never forget the time: I woke up in bed, I couldn't find my eyeglasses, and I thought they were wrapped up in the covers of the seemingly oversized "king-sized" bed. Unexpectedly, I later found them folded, lying next to my pillow.

This would repeatedly happen throughout the years. I was puzzled. I knew your Poppy Joey wasn't doing this. The bedroom door was locked. Bewildered, I decided to pray. I asked God to show me what was going on. The plan was to stay awake with my eyeglasses on and pretend to be asleep.

The next night, I was ready. I was positioned on my side of the bed, waiting with the blanket pulled up over my mouth. Although I was not scared, I was trembling. I felt hot breath on my face. It didn't feel human. I squinted my eyes, and what I saw was not Joey. I could see the outline of a big cat and his teeth! I wasn't startled. I knew my eyeglasses were being removed somehow. The evidence was now in front of my face. Mercy got closer. With his mouth, he took a hold of the bridge of my eyeglasses; pulling them off my face, he laid them down beside my pillow. He made them fold with his big front paw. "Mercy!" I shouted. "It was you all along!

CHAPTER ONE

Good Morning Abba Father!

"Good morning, Abba Father! Good morning, Joey, my hubby." My sound of enthusiasm broke through the snores and woke Joey up.

"Good morning, Carol, my wife. How are you?"

"I am Blessed! And how are you, my hubby? Manifestation! Finally, Mercy is going to Church today!"

It was Sunday, December 27, 2020. I was awoken by the alarm clock, and my dream was interrupted. I was taking Mercy, my beloved four-paw feline son, to church. My head was feeling foggy. I was thinking about the dream. I ran through the doorway towards Mercy's bed. "Good morning, Mercy Percy." I added in his middle name, which is Percy. I shouted, making sure I would have his full attention. "You're going to Church with Poppy and me today!"

He usually responds to my voice with his unusual "hmmm" or with his needy sound of "Mom-Mom," but this morning, he didn't. As I stepped back, I noticed things appeared strange because I hadn't put on my glasses.

"Wow!" Rejoicing and leaping with joy, I began to sing a song: "Mercy is going to Church today."

"Carol, Carol, don't get so excited. Did you ask Pastor about bringing Mercy to Church? You know some things – like pets – now have to be approved. You know the guidelines, Lynny (my nickname). You're the one who told me, even though he is Mercy," Joey chuckled.

"Oh My God, I repent!" When Joey calls me Lynny, I know I must have stepped out of line. I didn't get it approved by the Pastor. I had previously hinted to him about bringing Mercy to church, but Pastor Larry would always look at me and smile. Now it was too late to call the church's administrator. This is something I should have taken care of in my dream. Yes, in my dream! Then, it would have been okay. "Ha Ha Ha," I laughed out loud and chuckled for a minute. Then, disgusted, I said, "It's late. How am I going to be in church, on time? I have to finish getting dressed. Mercy Percy, how did Poppy get dressed so quickly? He's downstairs waiting for us."

I stood with my hand covering my mouth and started screaming, "The pet carrier!" I immediately ran downstairs and into the garage to find Mercy's pet-carrier. Found it! I grabbed the carrier and ran out of the garage. As I sat the carrier down on the coffee-table, Mercy's Poppy (my hubby) looks up from his morning cup of Joe.

"What are you doing, Carol? Are you okay?", he said.

Running up the stairs to finish dressing for Church, I replied, "Yes, it can't be any other feeling better than this, but to take Mercy to Church." As I stepped onto the last step of the stairs, I heard Joey chuckle.

"Oh Abba Father, Jesus, Holy Spirit, please help her. "

I shook my head, mumbling, "What's wrong with him?" Skipping to the bathroom, I thought about the ride to Church.

• CHAPTER TWO •

Kiss On the Cheek

Very excited now, I called out to Mercy every ten minutes. "Mercy, Mercy, we're going to Church! FLCF Church, here we come—my gray, blue-eyed, four-paw, feline son.

"Oh no," I muttered. My boots weren't sliding on. "It must be from all those delicious turkey-meatballs, potato-salad, kale, rolls, rice-pudding, and sweet-potato pie." I thought my feet had swollen after standing on them all night, and then eating that tasty food. "One more try with these boots," I said. "I don't want to change my outfit because it will make us arrive even later." I tried again. "One, two, three...it's on!" I bounced to my feet, grabbed my pocketbook, my book-bag, and walked over to pick up Mercy from his bed.

Mercy was still wrapped up in his special red blankie. He seemed to be all snuggled-up from his bath and a good brushing. There was no food or water left in his bowls. However, he never stuck his head out to give me a kiss on the cheek, nor to say "Mom-Mom." It seemed that Mercy was content and knew everything was alright because he was going to Church. It seemed he knew either that I should calm down, or he would just sleep so he wouldn't be nervous watching me.

"Here we go, Mercy-Mercy." Holding Mercy in my arms—close to my chest—I ran down the stairs. "My legs, Joey!" I complained. I thought, "this will be the last time for the steps before heading out to Church."

"Okay, Mercy; let me put you in your carrier, and away to Church we'll go." As I unzipped the top of the carrier, I realized Joey (Poppy) was sitting on the couch as though he was setting the laptop up for a meeting. I didn't ask him any questions about what he was doing. Instead, I grabbed the car-keys to warm up the car. "Joey, I'm going out to warm up the car!"

As I walked out the door—baffled how Mercy could be asleep through all my busyness—I stumbled over a bushel basket outside the door. To my surprise, it was filled with loaves of bread. Even though each loaf was individually wrapped, you could smell the fragrance of freshly made bread. Wondering, "Who left this?", I picked up the basket. There was a card lying beside it on the porch. "Hmmm, this must have fallen off the bushel," I thought. The card read:

"Manifestation, Be Blessed! Now, pick up your harvest—and because of the declarations that you have sown and are faithfully sowing, your house is now profoundly called "THE HOUSE OF BREAD." Each loaf can be distributed to your neighbors before 6 o'clock pm. Be a Blessing, Lynny!"

Chills ran up my spine. Inside me, I heard the word "Confirmation."

I shouted out to the neighbors that were standing on their porch, watching me, "This is what I've been talking about! This is just what my Pastor has been teaching in Church!"

9

"Church! Oh my God." We were late for church. I started the car and ran back into the house whilst carrying the bushel of bread. Joey looked up and stared at the container in my arms. He chuckled at me again.

"Where did you...? I'm not even going to ask," he said.

I was waiting for the car to warm up, and I began to prance the floor while singing: "Oh Lord, you're good...Oh Lord, you're good...Ohhh Lord, you're good and you're Mercy endureth forever! Oh Lord, you're good...Oh Lord, you're good...Ohhh Lord, you're so good and you're Mercy endureth forever!" After singing this one more time, I picked up my pocketbook, bookbag, and Mercy in his carrier. Finally, out the door, I hurried to get Mercy's carrier strapped into the seatbelt. It was hard to believe that Mercy was still asleep. Not once had he poked his head out of Blankie. Blankie is what we called his special red blanket that had pictures of different breeds of felines on it. I could hear Joey calling me from the door.

"Carol, are you okay?"

I was wondering why my husband didn't have his coat on. While sitting in the driver's seat, adjusting the heat, a sensation of joy and peace began to fill the atmosphere. The presence of joy was so strong. I felt strength increasing in my body. I shouted out to my feline passenger. "Mercy, are you okay? By now, you should have your praise on!"

Oh, yes! Mercy would get stirred up when he heard me praising the Lord. His tail would go up and down, slapping whatever surface he was near. He would sing along, making heavenly feline sounds of joyful praise.

"Jesus, Jesus," I shouted; realizing I was no longer in my driveway waiting for Joey to come out of the house. We were now at the Burger King traffic-light in Glassboro, New Jersey. A warm sensation of joy and peace had overtaken me. I had pulled off with the car and left Joey (Mercy's Poppy) and my cellphone. It was too late to turn around.

CHAPTER THREE

Pulling Up to the Church

Pulling up to the church, I noticed that no cars were parked in front or in the parking lot. Now I knew I was late. I couldn't call Joey or any of The FLCF members because I left my phone on the coffee-table. I laughed out loud. The powerless, ugly [s]atan was not going to steal my joy. I turned on the car. The clock showed 10:10am and service starts at eleven. A supernatural miracle has already manifested outside of the church building. Now, I'm smiling and declaring loud, "I am early!" I'm supposed to be early for every meeting. Still smiling, I thought, "It was 12:30 p.m. back at the house when I buckled the seatbelt around Mercy and his carrier. What a miracle. Thank you, Lord! I better give this testimony."

Another sensation began to flow from the top of my head until it reached the soles of my feet, but this time, it was hot. The joy and peace were so strong. I had a vision. I was sitting in a carrier—The Mercy Seat. I felt like running to get inside the church. I looked over at the church and could see a light on inside. "Mercy, Mercy. Maybe a custodian team-member left the door unlocked when he turned on the heater. Let's go, Mercy!" I said.

Jumping out of the car, I opened the passenger door, unfastened the seatbelt, and grabbed the carrier and my pocketbook; along with my bookbag. I had no choice but to shut the car door with my foot. I started to run. I was slowed down because of the carrier and the other baggage. The cold air was hitting my forehead and made me quite thankful for my mask. Thump, thump-thump, we went up the steep steps to try the door. "Oh no—it's locked! Buddy, your first day to church, we made it here, and we can't get in!"

Buddy was another nickname we sometimes called Mercy; especially when we would ask him for a "shake-shake," or when he would give us his paw to shake on his own. The shake would always prompt a pat on his head and an "Awe Buddy, I love you."

"Mercy, maybe I should look through the door window to see if I can see Brother Schmitt." Stooping, looking through the glass for Brother Schmitt, neither he, nor any of his team were visible. I shifted my body and stood up straight. The smell of fresh loaves of bread filled my nose again. It was so powerful. The fragrance was that of God's Love and Today's New-Morning Mercy—filling the atmosphere.

At this time, I needed a phone to call Joey to let him know where I was and what was going on. I began to turn around to face the adjacent college campus. Someone next door recognized me and was now shouting to get my attention. "Sister Lynny, Sister Lynny! Don't you know your Church is meeting on Zoom?"

"Oh my God!" I gasped. That's why Joey was sitting in front of the laptop and asking "Carol, are you okay?" Carol is what Joey calls me most of the time. It's short for my first name, Carolyn, which means—joy.

I began to rejoice on the steps with my praise dance. Mercy did come to Church today, although the door was locked. Down the steps, back in the car, pulling out of the parking lot, driving through Rowan University to Greentree Road, I begin to realize that Mercy was still asleep. The presence of the Lord was strong in the car. Again, the hot sensation begins to flow from the top of my head to the soles of my feet. I couldn't get my coat off. I had no choice but to turn the air conditioner on in the winter. I could hear the word "confirmation" inside me. I heard the same word at home that morning.

"Mercy, is that you? Mercy, is that you?"

He didn't respond with his "hmmm" or either his "Mom-Mom." I called him again.

"Mercy, Mercy, Mercy!"

Follow You All

T he voice, I could hear it softly. The same voice with the words I distinctly remembered hearing in my dream on Saturday night.

"MY MERCY ENDURES FOREVER. IT WILL FOLLOW YOU ALL THE DAYS OF YOUR LIFE. YOU HAVE TO PRESENT YOUR BODY AS A LIVING SACRIFICE; HOLY AND ACCEPTABLE IN MY PRESENCE WHERE YOU WILL ALWAYS FIND THE FULLNESS OF MY JOY. AND, IT HAD ALREADY BEEN GIVEN TO YOU AND WILL BE FOREVER AND EVER IN YOU.

MERCY, MERCY, MERCY IS MY GREATEST LOVE OF ALL. NOW, YOU HELP SOMEONE TO BELIEVE AND RECEIVE MY LOVE AND TRUST IN ME."

I pulled into the driveway. "Mercy we're home!" Hurrying around to the passenger side to open the door, I unbuckled the seatbelt, picked up my pocketbook, shouldered the bookbag, grabbed the carrier, shut the car door, walked to the porch, and into the house. "Whew!" I was smiling while saying, "Thank you, Lord Jesus, for safely bringing us back here!"

My arms were feeling so sore. I immediately sat the carrier with Mercy in it onto the coffee-table. There was Joey, Mercy's Poppy, still sitting in front of the laptop. I thought, "He must be online—joined in—on Zoom with Pastor Larry and FLCF." As I was taking off my coat, I could hear Pastor Larry closing out the service.

"Are you ready?" He was preparing us for our congregational confessions. "Be holy! Be filled with mercy." I was about to respond to the last declaration. I thought I heard another voice declaring loud along with me.

"I am filled with mercy!" The church, my husband, the voice, and I were harmonizing in agreement.

Joey looked up at me and said, "Where were you? You left your phone and didn't come back to get it. I was concerned because you had a lot on your mind and was rushing; circling around like a chicken with no head this morning."

"Joey, please stop there before you start those chicken jokes. This is not the time for them. And, I thought you were told this morning—this was the day Mercy was going to Church. I was so excited. At the same time, I didn't want to be late. I didn't realize I drove off without you. And, I forgot FLCF was not back in the building, but on Zoom until further notice. Someone next door recognized me while I was standing in front of the church door and told me."

As I hung up my coat, my intuition about Mercy prompted me to see about him because he was quiet all day. Although in denial, I ran to the carrier and slowly pulled back his red blankie. I said to myself, "the Holy Spirit's leadings are always right." My four-paw son—Mercy—wasn't wrapped in the blankie. "Oh, God! Where's my

Mercy?" Suddenly, I could hear the voice I heard earlier speaking to me again.

CHAPTER FIVE

Authority to Use My Power

"YOU WERE IN A HURRY, STILL THINKING OF THE DREAM THAT I GAVE YOU ABOUT A VISION AL-READY PLANNED FOR YOU AND THE WHOLE WORLD. I GAVE YOU A SPECIAL FOUR-PAW FELINE SON TO FOLLOW YOU AROUND FOR ALMOST 19 YEARS [APRIL 15, 2002.]. I THANK YOU FOR BEING OBEDIENT TO NAME HIM—MERCY. I CREATED HIM FOR YOU TO CHERISH. SO, WITH THIS PHYSICAL PET-CHILD, YOU WOULD BE REMINDED OF ME AND MY GREATEST LOVE—MY SON. NOW, YOU WILL HAVE TO CONTINUE STAYING IN MY WORD; TO BE STRONG IN ME AND IN MY MIGHTY POWER. KEEP YOUR ARMOR TIGHT EACH DAY SO THAT THE ENEMY'S INFLUENCES

WILL NOT STEAL, KILL, OR DESTROY YOU. HE WILL TRY TO SEND THOSE DARTS YOUR WAY. DO NOT RECEIVE THEM! YOU HAVE MY WORD. IT'S MY PERMISSION TO USE MY AUTHORITY AND MY POWER. MY THOUGHTS ARE THINGS THAT ARE OF PEACE AND NOT OF EVIL. WHAT THE DEVIL MEANT FOR EVIL WILL BE TURNED AROUND BY MY WORD.

"DO NOT LET MY WORD BE A MYSTERY IN YOUR BODY. IT'S AN ALREADY DONE DEAL. LET MY LIVING WATER CONTINUE TO RISE IN YOU AND OVERFLOW. JUST KEEP REJOICING UNTO ME. SING YOUR SPECIAL PSALMS; PSALMS 23, PSALMS 34, PSALMS 91, AND THE OTHER SPIRITUAL SONGS OF JOY, LOVE, AND PEACE. YOU HAVE FOUND PLEASURE IN KNOWING I'LL DO EXCEEDINGLY AND ABUNDANTLY ABOVE ALL THAT YOU ASK OR THINK, ACCORDING TO MY POWER THAT'S WORKING IN YOU. TRUST ME AT ALL TIMES WITH THE LONG, SATISFIED LIFE THAT I HAVE GIVEN YOU TO ENJOY. I WILL RETURN SOON FOR ALL MY PEOPLE. BE SURE OF

YOUR PURPOSE, AND CONTINUE TO HELP SAVE LIVES FOR ME. REMEMBER, I DID! AND IN ALL THINGS, GIVE ME THANKS AND PRAISE. THIS IS MY WAY OF PERFECTING HOLINESS AND TO ALWAYS REMIND YOU OF MY GOODNESS."

His Voice paused. He began to laugh, but I could hear as though three were laughing within one voice. The laughter was anointed. Smiling, I thought, some people would say it was contagious. I begin to laugh and laugh. I heard the voice I heard earlier. It was the Voice of One. God's voice pierced through my laughing. He began to distinctly speak to me again. This time, I was more relaxed because what I previously heard was penetrating through my body, breaking strongholds, tearing down walls, and uprooting all generational curses. Still, I was smiling as each word He spoke sounded like a roar of a lion, yet sufficiently full of grace.

Abba Heavenly Father God called me by my nickname. Some people do not like their nickname, I thought, chuckling. Although it gets your attention quicker. I guess Abba Daddy was making sure I was attentive and inclined to hear from now on.

"LYNNY, MY ANSWER TO YOUR QUESTION "WHERE'S MERCY?": HE'S IN YOUR HEART TODAY, TOMORROW, AND FOREVER, CAROLYN (JOY, AND A SONG OF HAPPINESS). MERCY DID COME TO CHURCH WITH YOU ON DECEMBER 27, 2020. THINK ABOUT IT.

"MY BELOVED, KEEP HEARING MY VOICE AND ALWAYS REMEMBER: I AM SO GOOD AND MY MERCY ENDURES FOREVER!"

O give thanks unto the Lord; for he is good: because his mercy endureth for ever.

PSALMS 118:1
THE HOLY BIBLE
(KJV)

• CHAPTER SIX •

The Day Mercy Went to Church (Poem)

This could have been an adventure
About the mall, park, or school.
Looking back on the days
When kids learned the golden rule.

Strange things I remember,
through the years I've seen pass.
From the days of forgetting homework
Or daydreaming in Sunday class.

Remembering fun with science
And learning mysteries in the sky.
Or feeling the heavenly presence
And asking questions—Why?

But I will never forget,
My brain do I search,
The one unfathomable day,
Mercy came to church.

I know you are thinking
What's so "strange with that?
Give me a minute to explain—
You see, Mercy is a cat.

Although a quite fitting allegory,
A cat with a tail and paws,
Could help religious saints to see
God's love in action working over laws.

It happened one Sunday morning.
The last bell on the church had rung.
The service had already started.
The choir had already sung.

Pastor Rick was ready to preach.
Quickly, he finished his prayer.
He turned his sermon over.
It was like no words were there.

Then Sister Convey hollered,
"I sense something new!"
But her face wasn't happy.
She seemed frustrated too.

"There is another presence!"
She said, "Someone brought him in here!"
The rest of the congregation gasp.
Others started to fear.

No one at first knew
To what she did refer.
She was staring at this basket
That had started to purr.

Then we saw something protruding
Out from under the lid,
Wagging so peaceful and happy,
I tell you that's what it did.

Ms. Convey became frantic.
She looked at deacon Steve.
"Get that thing out of here
Or I'm going to leave!"

"Not in our holy sanctuary
Can a feline creature be.
I can't have fur on my new blouse
The cleaners are not free!"

"It would be like that year
When the vicious family came
They tried to become members
Oh, what sin and shame!"

"Stuff like that will come on you.
Then before you know,
Our church will be filled with mess
And there will be no place to go."

It was tweenager Todgie Liles,
Who first pointed it out,
Taking up for the tail in the box
With a whisper-like shout.

And Todgie was persistent.
He now stood where he sat,
Shouting, "Jesus is the Lion of Judah
And a lion is just a big cat!"

THE DAY MERCY WENT TO CHURCH

It was Sister Joyce that brought him,
Everyone thought the same.
And she was the one who told us all
That Mercy was his name.

He was normally behaved,
So staying put she didn't doubt.
So she didn't tie down his carrier—
Only God knew Mercy would get out.

Pastor Rick was still speechless.
He didn't know what to say.
What does a pastor preach
When Mercy comes to church one day?

Then it started to happen.
At first, a trickle down one eye.
The Spirit of God started moving
And everyone began to cry.

Mercy had begun romping
Across the pews and down the isle.
And where tears weren't flowing,
There were the biggest smiles.

People were running to the altar
Fallings on their knees.
Suddenly, the place was shaking.
I thought I felt a breeze.

The pastor began to share
About Jesus on the tree.
That he died for everyone,
All sinners that we be.

Then the unthinkable happened
Right on Ms. Convey's lap.
Mercy jumped on her seat
As if to take a nap.

No one saw it coming.
It was amazing grace.
But, Mercy turned, stretched his legs
And kissed the sister on the face.

Her eyes were wide as valley pools
And her face dropped real long.
"Heavenly Father," she cried, "forgive me!
Oh, I've been so wrong!"

Mercy was more than a cat—
Sister Joyce to church did bring.
Mercy was Jesus loving us
Despite of all our sin.

Now our church is different
The doors are open wide.
From the streets you can feel it,
You see Mercy is still inside.

Oh, the day that Mercy came,
Showing up at our church door.
Reminding us, the Lord is good
And His Mercy will always endure!

—by Terrence for Carolyn

About the Author

Carolyn Cormina Clark-Joyce, AKA Lynny, and Lynnykins is a precious, big-hearted, gift made by God and two wonderful parents. She is a loving wife to her hubby, loving mother of two children, and mother to her feline pet "child." She is also a loving grandmother to five, a loving great-grandmother to four felines, a loving special great-grandmother to one canine, a loving sister to four siblings, a loving niece, a loving auntie, a caring cousin, a friend to many, and a devoted member of her church— Family Life Christian Fellowship.

Carolyn cherishes her most significant life success, which is her passionate, intimate relationship with her Heavenly Father, God. Her accreditations metaphorically include a BA (Born Again-Believer) MA (Made Available) Ph.D. (Praising Him Daily). She highly values being an Encourager and Helping Hand to many.

This book was published by:

The Glory Cloud publications LLC

P.O. Box 193

Sicklerville, NJ 08081

www.theglorycloudpublications.com

vof1@aol.com

For additional information about us and how to obtain other literature, or how to publish your life story, testimony, miracle report, biography, fiction, or children's story book, please write or email us at the above addresses.

Psalms 68:11

*Habakkuk 2:3, 4 *2 Corinthians 1-7 *Jude 22*

With our Voice and His Glory, by Faith